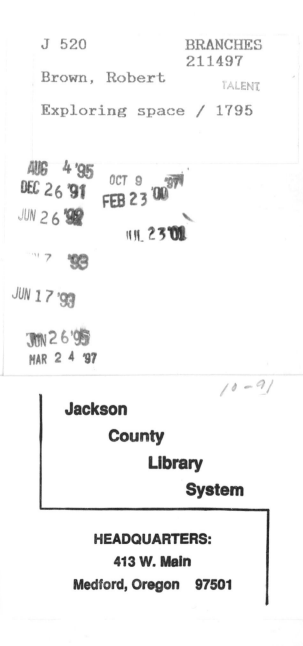

My First
REFERENCE LIBRARY

Exploring
SPACE

R. BROWN
B. JONES

Gareth Stevens Children's Books
MILWAUKEE

For a free color catalog describing Gareth Stevens' list of high-quality children's books call 1-800-341-3569

Library of Congress Cataloging-in-Publication Data
Brown, Robert, 1961-
    Exploring space / by Robert Brown and Brian Jones.
        p. cm. — (My first reference library)

    Includes index.
    Summary: A comprehensive guide for young readers to the mysteries
and marvels of the cosmos.
    ISBN 0-8368-0029-X
    1. Astronomy—Juvenile literature. [1. Astronomy.] I. Jones, Brian. II. Title.
III. Series.
QB46.B885   1989
520—dc20   89-11278

North American edition first published in 1990 by
Gareth Stevens Children's Books
RiverCenter Building, Suite 201
1555 North RiverCenter Drive
Milwaukee, Wisconsin 53212, USA

Photographic credits: Bernard Abrams, p. 29 (bottom); Chris Floyd, p. 31; NASA, pp.
14-15, 17, 20, 21, 25, 32-33, 40 (left), 47, 52 (left), 54; Copyright National Geographic Society,
paintings by Jean-Leon Huens, pp. 8, 9, 11, 34; Novosti, p. 46; Robert Harding Picture Library,
pp. 5, 6, 22, 29 (top), 32 (bottom); Royal Aeronautical Society, p. 7; Science Photo Library, pp.
10, 15, 23, 30, 40 (right), 44, 48, 49, 51 (left), 53, 58 (left); Chris Walker, p. 27 (top)

Illustrated by Julian Baum, Angus McKie (Young Artists), and Eugene Fleury

Cover illustration © Pat Rawlings, 1989

Series editors: Mark Sachner and Neil Champion
Research editor: Scott Enk
Educational consultant: Dr. Alistair Ross
Editorial consultant: Neil Morris
Design: Groom and Pickerill
Cover design: Kate Kriege
Picture research and art editing: Ann Usborne
Specialist consultant: Martin Wace

Printed in the United States of America

1 2 3 4 5 6 7 8 9 96 95 94 93 92 91 90

Contents

1: LOOKING AT SPACE

Our Place in the Universe

Earth in Space

Our Earth is just one of nine planets in our solar system that revolves around the Sun. Although the Sun seems large and bright, it is only an ordinary star. The Sun is one of billions of stars in the Galaxy. The

This is our solar system. The planets revolve around the Sun, which is at the center of the solar system. The planets vary in size, from Pluto (the smallest) to Jupiter (the largest). ▶

Light-years

Astronomers do not use miles or kilometers to measure how far away stars are. Instead, they use a unit of distance called a light-year. One light-year equals about six trillion miles (9.5 trillion km).

Our solar system

Uranus

Saturn

Pluto

universe consists of many clusters of galaxies.

Studying the Stars

Astronomers use many types of telescopes to study the night sky. Most telescopes magnify the light given off by stars, making them easier to see.

The night sky is a strange and interesting place. You do not need a telescope to study the stars. All you need to do is go outside on a clear night and look up at the sky.

▲This huge radio telescope detects radio waves given off by stars and other distant objects in space.

Jupiter

Venus   The Sun   Mercury

Earth

Mars

Neptune

5

The First Stargazers

Many ancient cultures made predictions by watching the stars. By watching for the star Sirius, the Egyptians predicted the flooding of the Nile. ▼

For thousands of years people believed that Earth was at the center of the universe. They also thought that Earth was flat, and that if you sailed to the horizon, you would fall off the edge! Today we know that our planet is round and orbits the Sun.

The Ancient Greeks

Several Greek astronomers felt that Earth was round and traveled around the Sun. Unfortunately, very few people listened to the ideas of these astronomers.

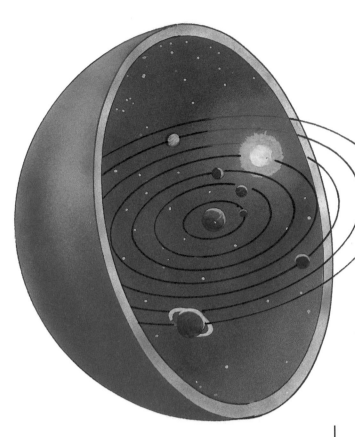

Sun
Mercury
Venus
Earth
Mars

Jupiter

Saturn

Uranus

Neptune

Pluto

◀ The picture on the left shows Ptolemy's Earth-centered universe. The picture above shows the correct order of the nine known planets around the Sun. ▲

Like most Greeks of his day, the astronomer Ptolemy believed that Earth was at the center of the universe. Ptolemy died in AD 180, and with him died ancient Greece's interest in the planets and stars.

Arabic Astronomy
A few hundred years after Ptolemy, the Arabs began studying the heavens. They drew accurate star charts that sailors used for navigation. But like the Greeks, they believed in an Earth-centered universe.

This Chinese star map shows the position of the stars in the sky. ▼

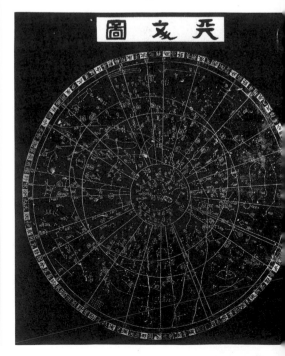

Changing Ideas

▲ Nicolaus Copernicus, a Polish astronomer, wrote a book in which he suggested that the planets orbited the Sun.

Nicolaus Copernicus

Ptolemy's idea of an Earth-centered universe was not really disputed until a book by Nicolaus Copernicus was published in 1543. In this book, Copernicus calculated that the Sun, not Earth, was at the center of the universe. Copernicus spent his life studying the movements of the planets.

Brahe and Kepler

Tycho Brahe (1546-1601) was a Danish astronomer. From his observatory off the Swedish coast, he made the most accurate observations of the stars and planets up to that time.

When Brahe died in 1601, his assistant, Johannes Kepler, continued Brahe's work. Kepler used Brahe's star charts to form his own idea of how planets moved. He showed that the planets' orbits were elliptical, or oval-shaped, rather than circular. His work correctly explained the motion of the planets.

Tycho Brahe's observatory

◀ Tycho Brahe was an excellent stargazer. In his observatory he made accurate charts of planetary motion.

◀ Johannes Kepler used mathematics to explain how the planets move. He discovered that planets move elliptically.

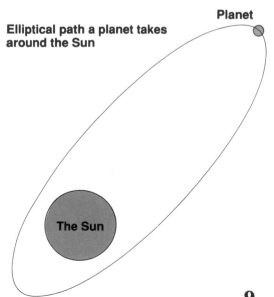

Elliptical path a planet takes around the Sun

Planet

The Sun

Telescopes

Kitt Peak National Observatory, Arizona. This observatory has one of the world's largest telescopes. ▶

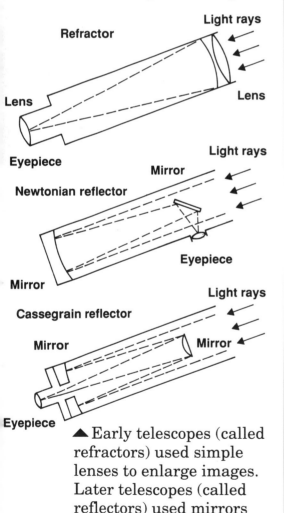

▲ Early telescopes (called refractors) used simple lenses to enlarge images. Later telescopes (called reflectors) used mirrors and lenses.

Early Telescopes

All telescopes help us see distant things more clearly. Galileo Galilei was the first astronomer who used telescopes to study the heavens. Galileo built refracting telescopes. His most powerful one could make an object appear 30 times larger.

In 1668, Isaac Newton invented the more powerful reflector telescope, which uses a mirror, instead of a lens, to collect light.

Astronomical Observatories

Large telescopes are kept in special buildings called observatories. The Kitt Peak National Observatory, located near Tucson, Arizona, is one of the largest in the world. Astronomers come to Kitt Peak from all over the world to study the stars for long periods of time. Most observatories are located in rural mountain areas, under dark, unpolluted skies.

▲ William Herschel (1738-1822) was an amateur astronomer. He discovered the planet Uranus in 1781, using a large telescope he had built.

Did You Know?

In 1789, William Herschel built a giant telescope. For many years, it was the largest in the world.

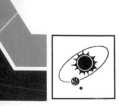

INTO SPACE

The Earth in Space

An illustration of Earth as seen by Apollo astronauts returning from the Moon. You can clearly make out North and South America. ▶

Pole Star

Direction of Earth turning

Equator

Axis

▲Earth spins on its axis, taking 24 hours (one day) to complete one revolution.

Earth takes one year, or about 365 days, to complete its orbit around the Sun.

The Seasons
Earth is tilted on its axis. In June, the Northern Hemisphere

tilts toward the Sun. It is then summer in the Northern Hemisphere and winter in the Southern Hemisphere. And in December, the situation is just the opposite, and the Southern Hemisphere tilts toward the Sun. It is then summer in the Southern Hemisphere and winter in the Northern Hemisphere.

The length of a planet's year depends on how long it takes to orbit the Sun. If you lived on Mercury, your year would last only 88 Earth days. On Pluto, the year is equal to 248 years on Earth!

At different times of the year, different parts of Earth tilt toward or away from the Sun. This tilt gives us our seasons. ▼

The seasons

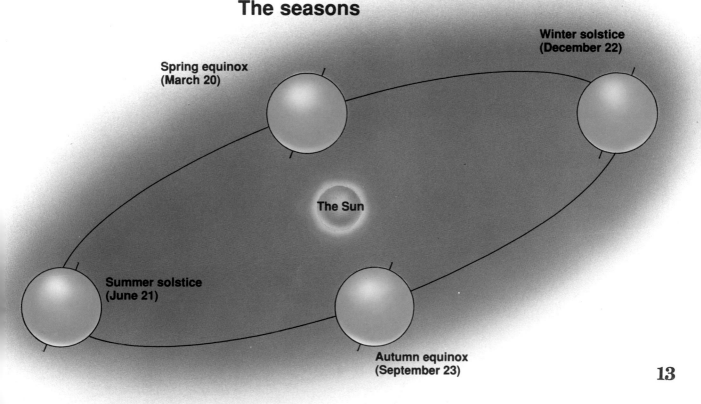

Spring equinox
(March 20)

Winter solstice
(December 22)

The Sun

Summer solstice
(June 21)

Autumn equinox
(September 23)

The Sun

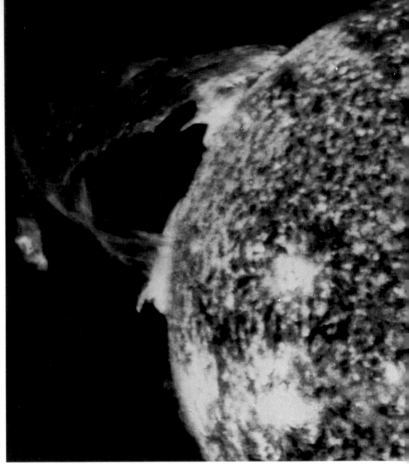

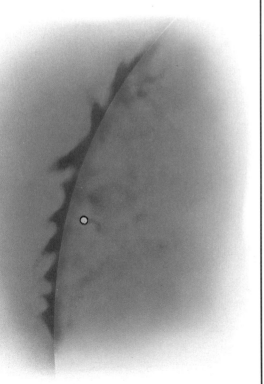

▲ The Sun is hot and huge. Its diameter is 100 times greater than that of Earth.

The Sun is a star. It seems much brighter than all the other stars because it is much closer to Earth. The Sun gives out energy in the forms of light and heat. Without this energy, there would be no life on Earth.

How the Sun Makes Energy

The Sun is not really burning. It produces energy by changing two atoms of hydrogen into one helium atom. When this occurs, a great deal of energy is produced. This special process is called nuclear fusion.

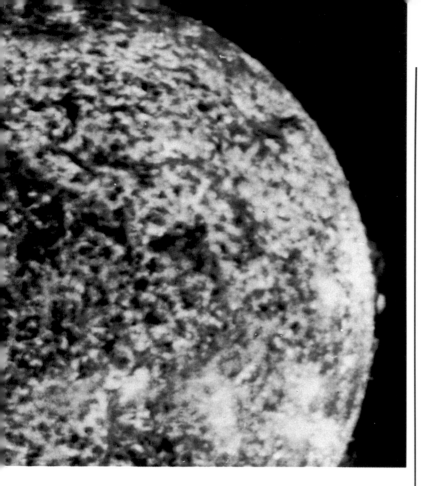

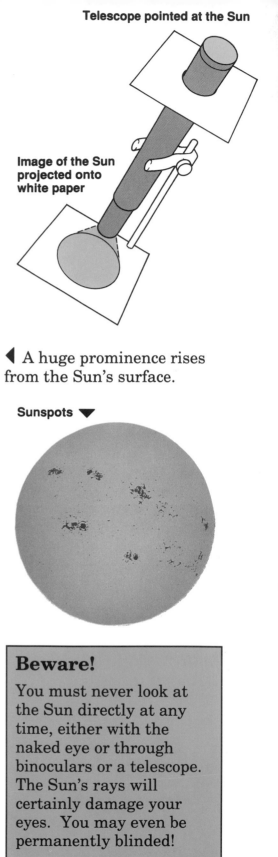

Image of the Sun projected onto white paper

◀ A huge prominence rises from the Sun's surface.

Sunspots ▼

Sunspots and Prominences

The Sun sometimes has dark patches on its surface called sunspots. These patches appear dark because they are cooler than the areas that surround them. Because the Sun turns on its axis, sunspots cross the Sun's face. Clouds of hot gas called prominences often rise above the surface of the Sun. Normally, special equipment is needed to view prominences, because they become lost in the Sun's glare.

Beware!

You must never look at the Sun directly at any time, either with the naked eye or through binoculars or a telescope. The Sun's rays will certainly damage your eyes. You may even be permanently blinded!

The Moon

This diagram shows the phases of the Moon. It takes 29 1/2 days for this cycle to be completed. The Moon appears to change shape because we can only see the lit portions from Earth.▶

Because the Moon has only one-sixth the gravity of Earth, people could jump much higher on the Moon than on Earth.▶

Moon Facts

• The Moon is about 239,000 miles (384,550 km) away from Earth. It is our closest neighbor in outer space.

• The Moon revolves around the Earth.

• The diameter of the Moon is quite small: 2,160 miles (3,475 km).

Earth's Satellite

The Moon is our closest neighbor in space. Astronomers have studied it for centuries, mainly through telescopes. More recently, space probes have landed on the Moon and carried out experiments on its surface. Because of all this, we know a great deal about Earth's satellite. The Moon has no atmosphere,

and from its surface the sky appears black.

The Surface of the Moon

The Moon is covered with light and dark areas. The light areas contain many craters. The dark areas are vast, flat plains, which early astronomers mistakenly thought were seas. The Moon's surface is very hot during the lunar day and very cold at night.

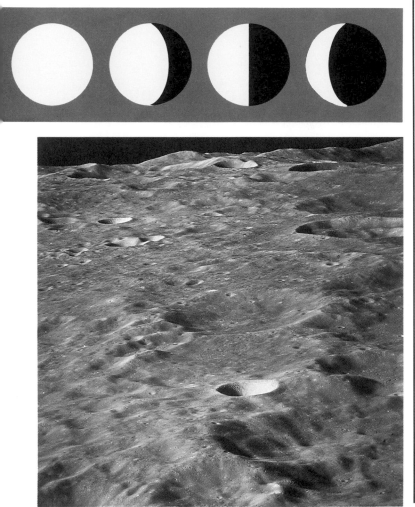

▲Astronauts on board the *Apollo 10* craft took this photograph of the far side of the Moon. The picture shows a rugged area with many craters.

◀ The Moon's surface.

Throughout the Moon's orbit, the same side always faces Earth. ▼

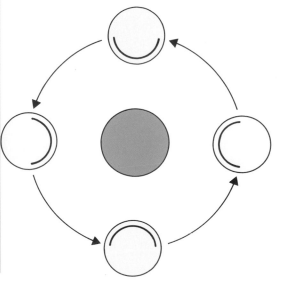

3: THE SOLAR SYSTEM

The Inner Planets

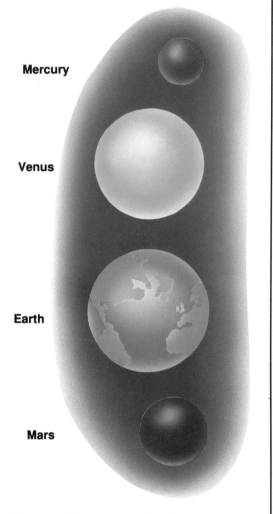

Mercury

Venus

Earth

Mars

▲ These are the four inner planets.

Astronomers place the known planets of our solar system into two main groups. One contains the four small, rocky inner planets. The other contains the four large outer planets that are made up mostly of gas. The final known planet, Pluto, is so far off that we know little about it.

Mercury
Mercury is the closest planet to the Sun. It has many craters as well as some mountains and flat areas. Since Mercury is hot enough to melt metals and has no atmosphere or water, it is unlikely that life exists on this small, moonless planet.

Venus
The next planet out from the Sun is Venus. Venus looks bright and beautiful from Earth, but it is covered by clouds of poisonous gases. These clouds block the sunlight from Venus's surface, but

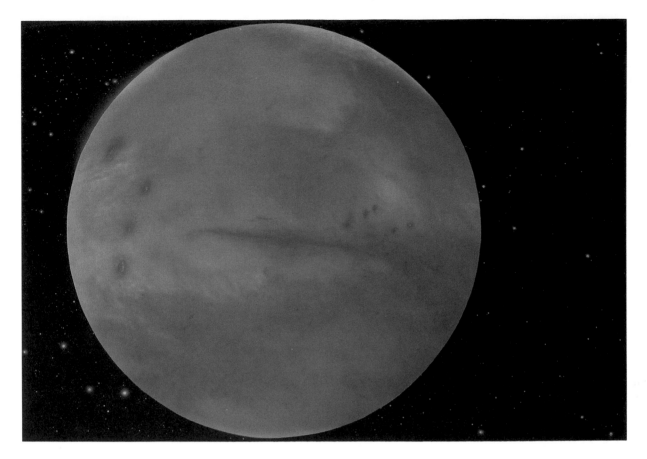

they also reflect sunlight, giving Venus its bright appearance. Venus also has a hot surface and volcanoes that may still be active.

Mars
Mars, the red planet, is the fourth planet from the Sun. Years ago, astronomers thought that Mars might have intelligent life. Many unpiloted space probes have visited Mars. They have found no signs of life on this cold, rocky planet.

▲This is a view of Mars, the red planet. Ancient astronomers named it after the god of war because it was the same color as blood. Mars has many spectacular features. At the left of this illustration, the largest brown spot is the volcano Olympus Mons, the tallest mountain in the solar system. The dark scar in the center of Mars is Valles Marineris, which is much deeper than the Grand Canyon on Earth.

The Outer Planets

Jupiter

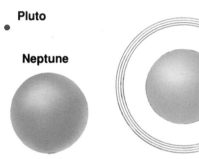

Pluto

Neptune

Uranus

Saturn

▲ The five outermost known planets of our solar system with an assortment of rings and moons.

In this photo of Jupiter, you can see the Great Red Spot, which is thought to be a gigantic storm. ▼

Jupiter and Saturn

Jupiter is the largest known planet in our solar system, and Saturn is the second largest. Like the other "gas giants," neither Jupiter nor Saturn has a solid surface. Each has colorful cloud belts that cross the planet. Both Saturn (with twenty-three) and Jupiter (with sixteen) have many moons.

Uranus and Neptune

Uranus, the seventh planet from the Sun, has faint rings. It has fifteen moons, but only five can

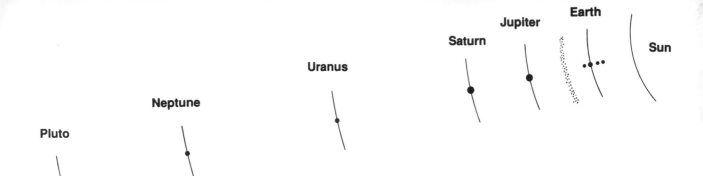

Pluto   Neptune   Uranus   Saturn   Jupiter   Earth   Sun

be seen from Earth. The rest were discovered by the *Voyager 2* spacecraft in 1986. Neptune is the most distant gas giant. During its 1989 visit, *Voyager 2* revealed Neptune's rings and several newly discovered moons.

Pluto

The outermost known planet is Pluto, a small and faint world. If there are planets beyond Pluto in our solar system, they will be quite difficult to detect.

▲These lines show partial orbits around the Sun of the five outer planets.

This is a photograph taken of Saturn from *Voyager 2*. Saturn's beautiful rings are made up of millions of tiny icy particles. You can see two moons, Rhea and Dione, as dots to the south and southeast.▼

Comets and Meteors

Comets are made up of water, ice, and dust. They are very small and cannot be seen when they are a long way from the Sun. As a comet nears the Sun, its ice melts, and the dust and gas that are released form a cloud, or coma. The coma is blown away by the Sun's energy. If there is enough dust and gas, the comet forms a tail.

Halley's Comet is the most famous of all comets. It was first recorded over 2,000 years ago. It orbits the Sun every 76 years. ▶

Minor Planets

These are tiny planetary bodies that were left over from when the solar system was formed. Most of us call them asteroids. Most asteroids orbit the Sun between Mars and Jupiter, though some move away from that region. Hidalgo travels out beyond Saturn, and the asteroid Icarus moves closer to the Sun than Mercury.

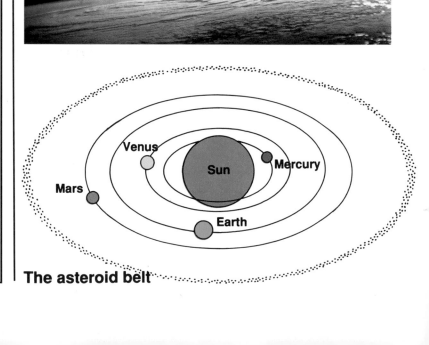

The asteroid belt

Meteors and Meteorites

A meteor is a streak of light that is a result of comet dust passing through Earth's atmosphere. Meteors are often called shooting stars, though they have nothing to do with stars. Sometimes large objects called meteoroids enter Earth's atmosphere and crash on the surface of our planet. Once meteoroids hit, they are called meteorites. When meteorites land they can cause craters like those on the Moon.

▲Arizona's Meteor Crater was formed when a huge meteorite hit Earth.

Particles burn up as they enter Earth's atmosphere.
▼

Eclipses

Eclipses of the Moon

We see the Moon because it reflects light from the Sun. A lunar eclipse takes place when the Moon passes through Earth's shadow. During a lunar eclipse, the Moon's surface becomes quite dark. Lunar eclipses occur more often than solar eclipses.

This illustration shows a full lunar eclipse. When this happens, Earth casts a shadow over the Moon. This diagram is not drawn to scale. Actually, the Sun is over 100 times as wide as Earth. ▼

Eclipses of the Sun

Although the Sun is much bigger than the Moon, it is also much farther away. That is why they look the same size in the sky. If the Moon gets between the Sun and Earth we see a solar eclipse. Because the Moon orbits Earth once a month, you may think a solar eclipse should occur every month. But since the path of the Moon is tilted, it "misses" the Sun almost every time. When the Moon gets exactly between the Sun and Earth, we have a total eclipse. When this happens, the sky becomes quite dark and stars can be seen. Total eclipses are very rare.

Did You Know?

Many people have believed that eclipses are magical. The ancient Chinese thought solar eclipses were caused by a dragon eating the Sun. People would then beat gongs and drums to scare the dragon away.

4: THE UNIVERSE BEYOND

The Stars

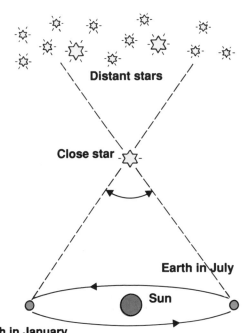

Distant stars

Close star

Earth in July

Sun

Earth in January

▲These diagrams show how you can use an object that is fairly close at hand to measure objects farther away. To do this, you need to compare the angle of a closer object at a known distance with the angle of an object that is farther away. ▶

Constellations

At first glance, the night sky appears to be a jumbled mass of stars. From earliest times, people have looked at those stars and found patterns, or constellations. The stars in a constellation are not really close together. They all lie at different distances from Earth and only seem close to each other. There are a total of 88 constellations. Some, like Orion (the Hunter) and Ursa Major (the Great Bear), are easy to locate. Others are small and faint.

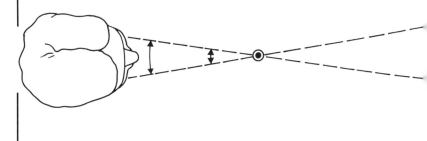

Distances of the Stars

The German astronomer Friedrich Bessel was the first to measure the distance of a star from Earth. He found that a star in the constellation of Cygnus (the Swan) was 11 light-years away. For very distant stars, astronomers compare their brightness with closer stars. Each star has its own color. Some of the brighter ones, like orange-red Betelgeuse or brilliant white Sirius, can be seen with the naked eye. The color of a star tells us about its general condition, age, and temperature.

◀ Star Brightness

The stars appear to have different brightnesses. The brightness of a star (or of another object in the sky, such as a planet) is known as its magnitude. The lower the number, the brighter the star. For instance, the faintest stars visible to the naked eye have a magnitude of 6, while bright stars have a magnitude of 0. Very bright stars have a minus number. The star Sirius, in Canis Major (the Great Dog), is the brightest star in the sky besides the Sun. It has a magnitude of -1.4. ▼

The Life of a Star

Stars are born inside giant clouds of gas and dust called nebulae. Parts of the cloud collect together and form a star. As the star shrinks, it becomes very hot and, like our Sun, produces heat and light. When the star's fuel is used up, the star changes. It turns into a red giant. This will happen to Earth's Sun — but not for a very long time. Later, the star will collapse and form a white dwarf. A white dwarf is so

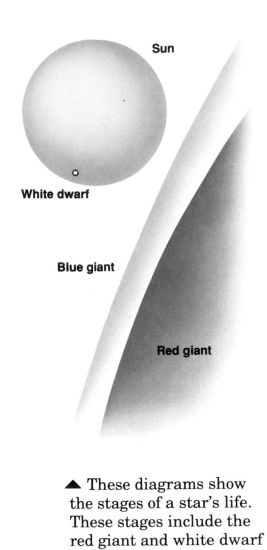

Sun

White dwarf

Blue giant

Red giant

▲ These diagrams show the stages of a star's life. These stages include the red giant and white dwarf stages. ▶

dense that even only a cupful of its material may weigh many tons! Eventually a white dwarf turns into a cold, dark globe.

Some stars use up their fuel at a very quick rate and explode. These exploding stars, called supernovas, propel beautiful clouds of the star's material out into space. The center of a supernova collapses and forms a neutron star. Just a spoonful of neutron-star matter would weigh billions of tons!

▲Above: the remains of a supernova. Below: the double star Albireo. ▼ Double stars may look like one star but are really two.

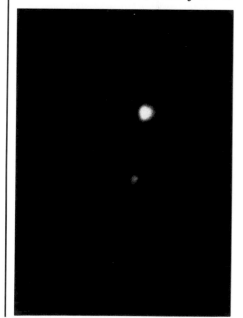

Nebulae and Star Clusters

Nebulae

Nebulae are clouds of gas and dust. Some nebulae are dark. But many are bright, because they are lit up by stars inside them. Some nebulae are visible with the unaided eye. One of these is the Orion Nebula.

Star Clusters

The gas inside the Orion Nebula is collecting to form new stars. Eventually, the cloud will collapse and form a star cluster. There are two types of star clusters: open clusters and

▲ Views through a telescope of the Orion Nebula (above), and the Pleiades (right), a young open star cluster. ▶

30

globular clusters. Open clusters, also known as galactic clusters, are loose collections of stars with no definite shape. These clusters can contain anything from a dozen to many hundreds of stars. Our Milky Way Galaxy (see pages 32-33) contains many star clusters.

▲The Lagoon Nebula is a large gas cloud in which stars are forming. A cluster of young stars can be seen inside the nebula.

Globular Clusters

These are large star clusters that are ball- or globe-shaped. They contain thousands or even millions of stars.

◀ Tucanae is a huge globular cluster with thousands of stars.

Galaxies

Quasars

Quasars are among the most distant objects that we have seen. They lie at the edge of the universe. Is there an end to the universe? Or does it stretch on forever? One day we may find out.

The Milky Way Galaxy

On a clear night you can see a misty band of light stretching across the sky. This is the Milky Way. Our Galaxy is shaped like a giant pinwheel, with spiral arms coming out from a central bulge. Our Sun is about two-thirds of the way out from the Galaxy's center. Our Galaxy is a member of a cluster of galaxies. This cluster is known as the Local Group, which is made up of more than twenty other galaxies.

This picture of the Milky Way Galaxy shows the combined light of thousands of stars. The streak of light is the trail left by an artificial satellite. ▶

This is an edge-on view of a spiral galaxy similar to the Milky Way. A band of stellar dust runs across the galaxy. The bright center of the galaxy is called the nucleus. ▶

The Expanding Universe

The universe came into being billions of years ago. This may have been because of a huge explosion, called the Big Bang, which released matter into space. This matter then formed galaxies, planets, stars, and everything that we know exists. Most scientists think that the universe is still expanding from the Big Bang.

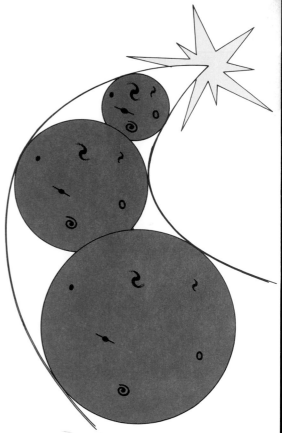

▲The Big Bang Theory: A huge explosion gave birth to the universe.

▲Galaxies come in many different shapes.

◀ The Andromeda Galaxy: the Milky Way's galactic "neighbor."

33

Finding the Pole Star

▲ This illustration shows how to find the Pole Star by using the Pointers in Ursa Major. The inset shows the double star Alcor and Mizar.

Galileo stargazing. ▶

Ursa Major (the Great Bear) is a large constellation. Most of its stars are quite faint. But the seven brightest are arranged in a pattern you can easily recognize. These seven stars are known as the Big Dipper. The two stars at the end of the Big Dipper are often called the Pointers. If you follow an imaginary line from the Pointers, you will come to the Pole Star. This is the brightest star in Ursa Minor (the Little Bear), which contains the Little Dipper. Earth's axis points directly to the Pole Star.

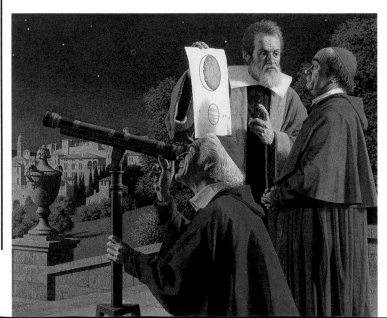

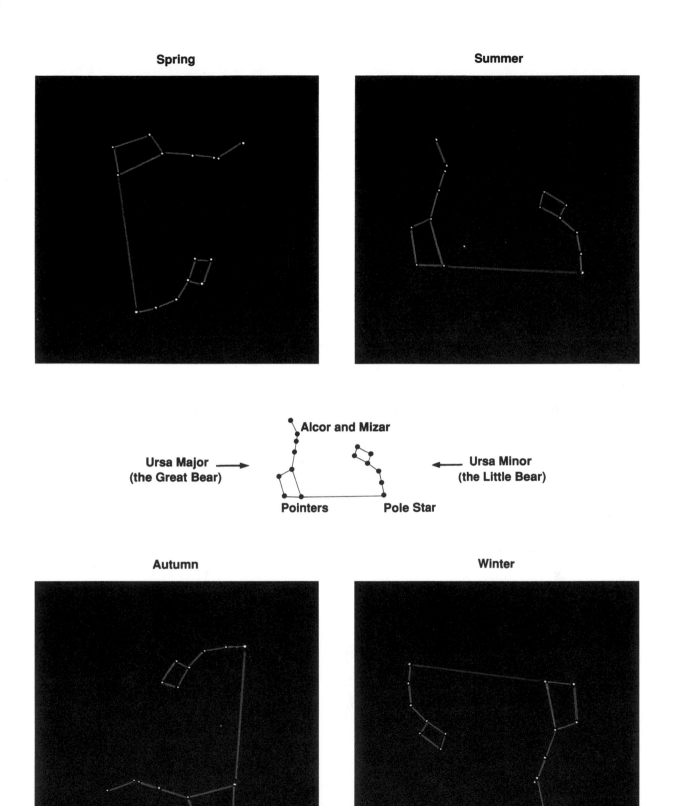

Spring

Summer

Alcor and Mizar

Ursa Major ⟶
(the Great Bear)

⟵ Ursa Minor
(the Little Bear)

Pointers

Pole Star

Autumn

Winter

The Southern Cross

The Southern Cross: This constellation can only be seen from the Southern Hemisphere. ▼

The Pole Star can only be seen from the Northern Hemisphere. However, people in the Southern Hemisphere have their own constellations, some of which cannot be seen from the north. One of the most famous southern star groups is Crux (the Cross), which is also known as the Southern Cross. Quite close to Crux lies the constellation Centaurus (the Centaur).

The Southern Cross

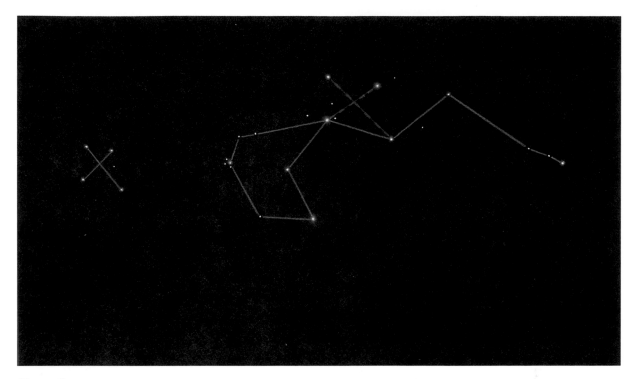

Carina

Carina was once part of a much larger constellation called Argo Navis. It represented the ship in which Jason and the Argonauts (characters from ancient Greek mythology) sailed in search of the Golden Fleece. During autumn evenings in the Southern Hemisphere, Carina (the Keel) can be found high in the southwestern sky. Its brightest star is Canopus, which is the second brightest star in the entire sky. Spacecraft use this brilliant white star for navigation.

▲Carina: This constellation lies close to the Southern Cross (pictured on the left). Carina was once part of Argo Navis, a constellation that represented the *Argo*, a ship in Greek mythology.

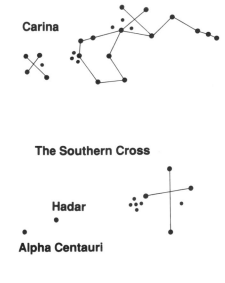

Carina

The Southern Cross

Hadar

Alpha Centauri

Stars and Myths

Many ancient peoples looked up at the stars and made patterns out of what they saw. They named the shapes after people, animals, gods, and objects like boats or musical instruments. Today we still use many of the names the ancient Greeks gave the stars. Here are just a few examples of these.

In the center of this group of stars you can see the Square of Pegasus. Andromeda can be found above Pegasus, to the left. The lower diagram on page 39 identifies the various stars of Pegasus and Andromeda. ▼

Andromeda and Pegasus

In the Northern Hemisphere, Andromeda and Pegasus are the main autumn constellations. You can see them high up in the southern sky during October and November evenings. In Greek mythology, Andromeda is a

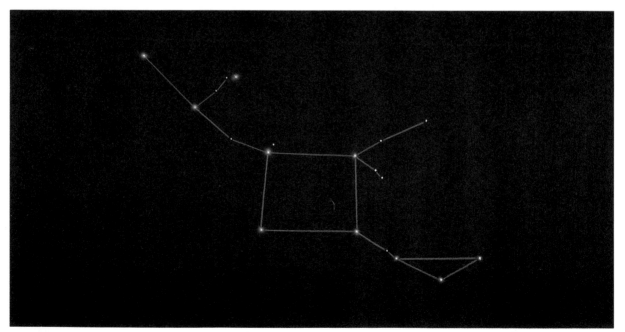

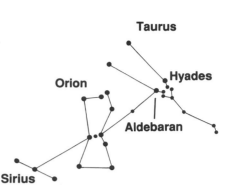

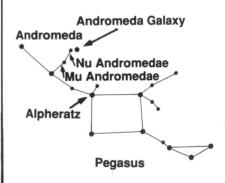

beautiful maiden who was rescued from a sea monster. The constellation Andromeda contains the most distant object visible to the naked eye: the Andromeda Galaxy (see "Galaxies," pages 32-33).

Pegasus is named after the winged horse of Greek mythology. The four main stars of the group form the Square of Pegasus. When seen on a star map, the square looks quite bright. But most of the stars making up the square are fairly faint, and you may have trouble finding it in the night sky.

◀▲ Here you can see Orion in the center of the picture. The Belt of Orion acts as a pointer down to Sirius, the brightest star in the constellation of Canis Major (the Great Dog). The Belt of Orion also points up to Aldebaran, a bright star found in the constellation of Taurus (the Bull).

▲ Pegasus and Andromeda join up at the shared star Alpheratz. To the right of Nu Andromedae is the spiral Andromeda Galaxy (see also page 33).

Into Space and Back

▲ The July 1969 launch of the first piloted Moon flight, *Apollo 11*, with US astronauts Edwin Aldrin, Neil Armstrong, and Michael Collins on board the craft. ▶

The Countdown

When a spacecraft launch is shown on television, the countdown usually goes from ten down to one and liftoff! But it takes much longer than this.

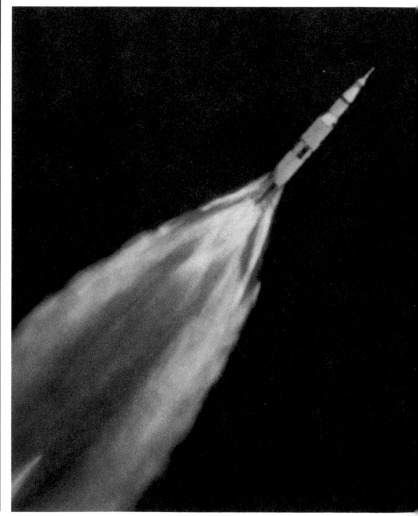

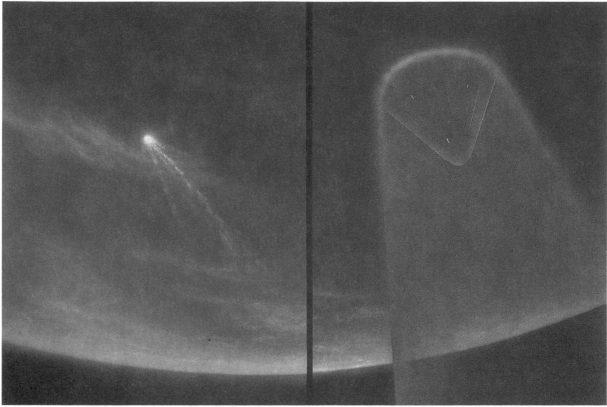

▲These pictures show two ways spacecraft return to Earth.

During the entire countdown, computers constantly check the spacecraft for possible problems.

Orbit and Return to Earth
Once a spacecraft escapes our planet's atmosphere, it enters Earth orbit. Eventually, piloted craft return safely to Earth. But many unpiloted satellites undergo orbital decay. This means they are slowly pulled back into the atmosphere and burn as they fall to Earth.

Different Orbits
The type of orbit a spacecraft uses depends on its mission. Television and communications satellites travel around Earth once every 24 hours in the same direction as Earth's rotation. This means they stay above the same point on Earth's surface. Weather satellites travel over the North and South poles, so they will pass over a different region during each orbit.

Unpiloted Space Flights

An artist's concept of a view of Earth from space. You can see the swirling clouds moving over land and sea. ▶

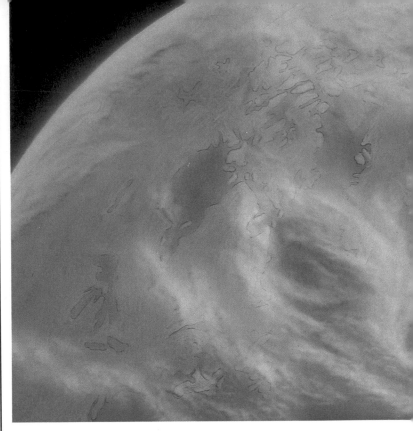

Sputnik 1, the first artificial satellite, was launched on October 4, 1957, by the Soviet Union. ▼

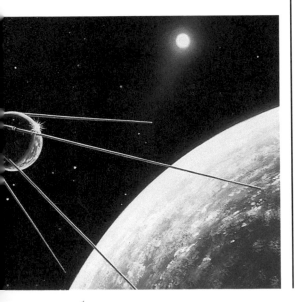

With a crew on board, reentry to Earth is controlled. Rockets bring the vehicle down into the atmosphere, and in order to protect the craft and crew, special heat shields are built into the craft so it will not burn up. Generally, spacecraft make their final descent by parachute, although the space shuttle glides down to Earth like a huge, unpowered aircraft.

Unpiloted Satellites

The first artificial satellite, *Sputnik 1*, was launched by the Soviet Union in 1957. This

Astronomers use satellites to carry out observations from space. This satellite recorded ultraviolet energy given off by stars.

marked the beginning of the Space Age. Satellites are used for many purposes, including weather forecasting, spying, communications, astronomy, and Earth observation. Weather satellites play an important role in weather forecasting. From high above Earth, satellites tell us a great deal about wind patterns and cloud movement. Astronomers also use satellites to carry special instruments above the atmosphere, where they make observations that are difficult or impossible to do from the ground.

Space Telescopes

A somewhat unusual "satellite," the Hubble Space Telescope, will be launched in 1990 from the space shuttle. This large telescope will enable astronomers to see farther into space than ever before. They will see objects that are fifty times fainter and seven times farther away than they can now detect.

Space Suits

▲ A shuttle astronaut wearing the Manned Maneuvering Unit high above Earth.

What Is a Space Suit?

A space suit is special clothing designed to protect astronauts from such dangers as changes in temperature, harmful rays from the Sun, fast-moving space dust, and the vacuum of space, where there is no oxygen. It takes many months to make a space suit. Each part must be tested thoroughly and then assembled and tested again. This assures that the space suit will stand up to the wear and tear of a space mission. On the back of the suit is a backpack called the Primary Life-Support System (PLSS). On Earth, it weighs close to 250 lbs (115 kg); away from the pull of Earth's gravity, it weighs nothing.

The Manned Maneuvering Unit

The Manned Maneuvering Unit (MMU) is a special backpack. It allows astronauts to "space walk" away from the craft. The MMU has small jets that enable astronauts to steer through space in any direction.

Space suit and Manned Maneuvering Unit

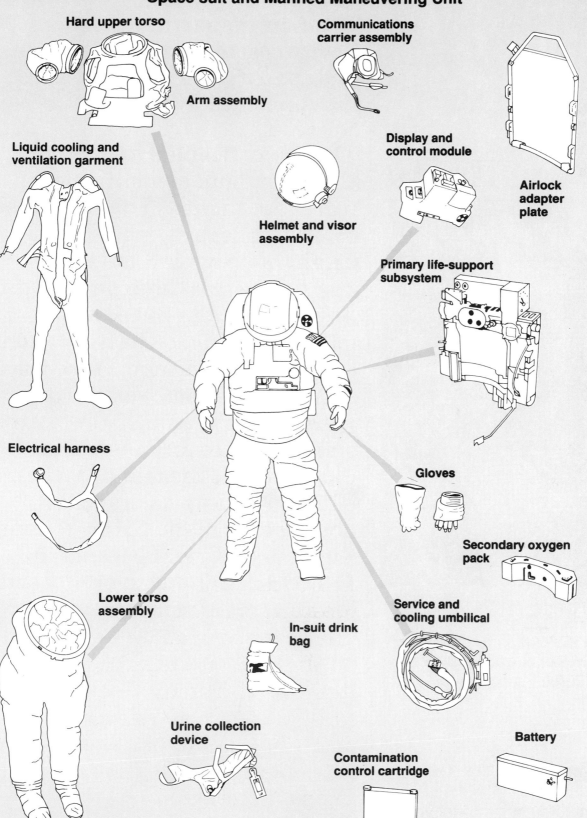

Hard upper torso

Arm assembly

Communications carrier assembly

Liquid cooling and ventilation garment

Helmet and visor assembly

Display and control module

Airlock adapter plate

Primary life-support subsystem

Electrical harness

Gloves

Secondary oxygen pack

Lower torso assembly

In-suit drink bag

Service and cooling umbilical

Urine collection device

Contamination control cartridge

Battery

Early Piloted Space Flights

▲ The first woman in space was Soviet cosmonaut Valentina Tereshkova. She orbited Earth 48 times in *Vostok 6* in June 1963.

Soviet cosmonaut Yuri Gagarin was the first human to go into space. He orbited Earth once in *Vostok 1* in April 1961. ▶

The first human in space was the Soviet cosmonaut Yuri Gagarin. His spacecraft, named *Vostok 1*, was launched in April 1961.

The Next Steps into Space

US astronauts made the next two space flights. The first was by Alan Shepard, who flew to a height of about 116 miles (187 km) before splashing down in the Atlantic Ocean. Shepard was followed by Virgil Grissom and by cosmonaut Gherman Titov, who orbited Earth for over one day. During his mission, Titov suffered space sickness. This is like travel sickness and can be one of the more unpleasant things about space flight. After Titov's flight, John Glenn became the first US astronaut to orbit Earth.

First Space Walk

The USSR launched the first three-person crew on board *Voskhod 1* in October 1964. This was a very dangerous mission because the spacecraft was designed for only one person. Luckily, the flight was successful. A half-year later, *Voskhod 2* was launched carrying two cosmonauts. Aleksei Leonov carried out the first space walk during this mission.

◀ During the *Gemini 4* mission in June 1965, Ed White became the first US astronaut to walk in space.

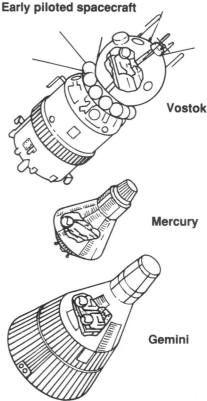

Early piloted spacecraft

Vostok

Mercury

Gemini

The Gemini Program

The US Gemini craft were made to carry two people into space. US astronauts began to make much longer space flights and carried out a number of space walks. The steps taken during these flights helped pave the way for the later Apollo missions, including those that put people on the Moon.

The Moon Landings

Disaster Strikes!

Disaster struck on the *Apollo 13* flight. On its way to the Moon an oxygen tank exploded in the service module. The loss of electrical power put the lives of the crew in danger. The astronauts transferred to the lunar module and used it as a "lifeboat." Happily, to the relief of a waiting world, they made it back to Earth.

This view shows the lunar rover and lunar module on the Moon's surface during the *Apollo 15* mission. In the background you can see lunar mountains. ▶

The Early Flights

The first Apollo flights prepared for the first Moon landing. *Apollo 8* took men to the Moon and back for the first time. The astronauts flew around the Moon but did not actually land. *Apollo 10* flew to the Moon, where the lunar module separated from the main spacecraft. The lunar module then descended to within a few miles of the Moon's surface.

Walking on the Moon

The *Apollo 11* mission took place in July 1969. The three astronauts were Neil Armstrong, Edwin Aldrin, and Michael Collins. It took three days to reach the Moon. After orbiting twelve times, the lunar module separated with Armstrong and Aldrin aboard. Once the module touched down, Neil Armstrong climbed down the ladder on the side of the module and became the first person to walk on the Moon.

▲During the *Apollo 11* mission, US astronaut Edwin Aldrin stands on the Moon's surface next to a "waving" US flag. His footprints are in the lunar soil.

The Lunar Rover

On the final three Moon missions, astronauts took with them the lunar rover, a kind of "Moon car." It enabled the astronauts to explore large areas of the Moon. They drove the rover over almost 60 miles (100 km) of the Moon's bumpy terrain.

The Space Shuttle

This space shuttle uses a special robotic arm to repair a satellite in orbit. ▶

What is the Space Shuttle?

The space shuttle is a reusable spacecraft that is launched into space like a rocket and returns to Earth like a huge glider. And since the shuttle is reusable, it has greatly reduced the cost of space flight. ▼

Uses of the Space Shuttle

The space shuttle has many uses. It can carry satellites into orbit, bring them back to Earth, or repair them in space. Satellites and other scientific equipment are carried in a special compartment called the payload bay. Once the shuttle is in orbit, the two large doors that cover the payload bay are opened, exposing it to space.

Launch and Return to Earth

The main part of the shuttle is the orbiter. This is the section that contains the flight deck, living quarters, and payload bay. A shuttle flight is controlled by the commander and pilot astronaut, with help from a team back on Earth. The shuttle orbiter has four engines. The two larger engines are used during takeoff. The two smaller engines are used to lift the orbiter into orbit and return it to Earth's atmosphere. When the orbiter returns to Earth, it glides silently down through the atmosphere and lands like an aircraft on a long runway.

This is the shuttle taking off. It carries a large fuel tank and two extra boosters to give it the power to launch itself. The boosters are ejected after about two minutes. ▼

Shuttle launch   Ejecting boosters   Ejecting the fuel tank

THE FUTURE

Probes to the Planets

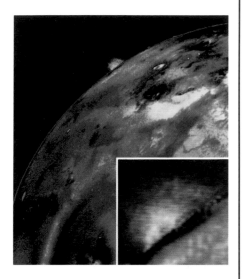

Before the Space Age, astronomers could do little more than look at the Moon and planets through telescopes here on Earth. All of this changed when Earth began sending space probes to other planets in the solar system.

Missions to the Moon

The first pictures of the Moon's far side were taken in 1959 by the Soviet *Luna 3* spacecraft. Since then, many space probes have been sent to the Moon. Some have even landed on the surface and brought lunar soil back to Earth.

Voyager

A number of probes have been sent to explore the outer planets. The best-known of these are the US Voyager craft. *Voyager 1* and *2* have shown us a great deal about Jupiter, Saturn, Uranus, and Neptune. For now, no trips to Pluto are scheduled.

Pioneer flies by Venus. ▶

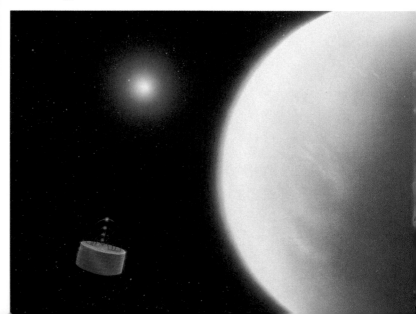

Exploring the Planets

Space probes have visited every planet but Pluto. The only flight to Mercury was made by the US *Mariner 10* craft, which flew past the planet three times in 1974 and 1975, taking thousands of pictures of Mercury's surface. Because of Venus's dense clouds, the many probes that have either flown past or gone into orbit around the planet could not photograph its surface. The Soviet *Venera 9* was the first probe to land on Venus and beam back pictures from the surface of another planet.

▲This photo was taken by the US *Viking 1* on Mars in 1976. Part of the probe is visible in the corner of the picture. Future probes will explore other bodies in our solar system, such as Pluto, comets, and asteroids.

◀ Opposite, left: Voyager sent back these photos of a volcano erupting on Io, one of Jupiter's moons.

Looking at Mars

The first successful mission to Mars was by the US *Mariner 4* craft. It flew past Mars in 1965 and sent back over twenty pictures of the surface of Mars.

Space Stations

A space station is a place where astronauts and scientists live and work. As space stations orbit Earth, scientists can conduct experiments that would be impossible to do on Earth because of gravity. Space stations get their power from solar panels that turn sunlight into electricity.

Salyut, Skylab, and *Mir*

The first space station was the Soviet *Salyut 1*, which was launched in 1971. In 1973, the

▲ This is *Skylab* orbiting Earth at a height of over 250 miles (400 km). One of its solar panels fell off during liftoff.

This is how a scientist pictures a space shuttle docking with a future space station. ▶

▲The Soviet *Mir* space station was launched in 1986.

United States launched *Skylab*, which stayed in space until 1979. The latest Soviet space station is called *Mir*. It will be used for studying the universe and doing medical research. A large US space station is also being planned. The parts for it will be made on Earth and then ferried into space and assembled. The station will have a number of uses, such as repairing satellites.

Colonies on Other Planets

One day observatories may be built on the Moon. Since the Moon has no atmosphere, astronomers will be able to see more distant stars. ▼

Lunar Bases

The first space colonies will probably orbit Earth. In time, colonies may be built away from Earth, starting on the Moon. The Moon is rich in minerals and could provide materials to build colonies. Farms could be set up using lunar soil to grow crops.

Colonies on Other Planets

Most planets in the solar system are too hot or do not have solid surfaces on which to build bases. But colonies might be built on

Mars, some of the asteroids, and the moons of other planets.

Travel to the Stars

One day, far in the future, people may travel to the stars. The rockets we have today would take thousands of years to reach even the nearest stars, so faster spaceships will be needed to settle deep space.

▲These Moon settlers are taking rock samples to analyze back at their base.

People living in space colonies for long periods of time will have to produce their own food. ▼

Alien Life

The Search for Alien Life
There are billions of stars in our Galaxy and billions of other galaxies. Many astronomers

Did You Know? ▲

We humans have been sending radio signals into deep space for several years. One message was sent in 1974 from the huge radio telescope in Arecibo, Puerto Rico. It was beamed toward a distant cluster of stars. But since these stars are so far away, it will take thousands of years before our message gets there. And who knows if anyone out there will receive — or return — our message?

Is there alien life on some other planet in the universe? This is an artist's idea of beings living on another planet.

Pioneer 10 has left the known solar system behind. It carries on board a plaque designed to explain many things about humans to any alien life that may come across it. ▼

believe intelligent life may exist on planets going around other stars. Some scientists are trying to contact alien civilizations, but their chances of success are small.

What Would Aliens Look Like?

If we did find other beings in the vastness of space, what would they be like? The answer to this question would depend on what the conditions were like on their home planet. They may have furry bodies, strange skin, or large eyes. Whatever they do look like, they will be different from us humans on Earth. How different? Until we make contact and see for ourselves, we can do little more than guess.

◄ Opposite: Will Earth colonies on other worlds make contact with alien life?

Glossary

Alien: A being or creature who comes from elsewhere, such as another country or another planet.

Asteroid: One of a number of small planet-like objects, most of which orbit the Sun between Mars and Jupiter.

Astronomer: A person who studies the universe and the objects in it.

Atmosphere: The layer of gas surrounding an astronomical body.

Atoms: Tiny particles from which all substances are made.

Axis: An imaginary line through an object around which it spins.

Colonies: Places where people from other places settle and live. Early settlers started colonies in North America. In the future, people from Earth may start colonies in space.

Comets: Clumps of ice, gas, and dust orbiting the Sun. When they get close to the Sun, the Sun's heat makes a comet throw off gas and dust, which form the comet's tail.

Constellation: A pattern of stars in the sky. There are now 88 recognized constellations.

Cosmonaut: The Soviet term for astronaut.

Crater: A pit or hole in the Earth, Moon, or some other astronomical body caused by the impact of a meteorite.

Density: The amount of something that exists in a given space. The more dense something is, the more it will weigh than the same volume of something less dense. For example, liquid water has a greater density than air. (See **Volume**.)

Ellipse: A shape similar to an oval. The orbits of the planets as they go around the Sun are elliptical.

Equator: An imaginary line running around the Earth (or any other astronomical body) midway between its poles.

Galaxies: Gigantic collections of stars, many of which also contain gas and dust. Galaxies can be any of a number of different shapes. Our own Galaxy, of which the Sun is a member, is shaped somewhat like a huge pinwheel.

Gas: A substance, like air or steam, which is not solid or liquid.

Gravity: The force which holds objects to the Earth, or to any other astronomical body. Gravity is what keeps the planets in orbit around the Sun.

Helium: The second most common substance in the universe. It is usually found in the form of a gas.

Hemisphere: Literally "half-sphere"; a half of the Earth or other astronomical body. The equator divides Earth into the Northern and Southern hemispheres.

Hydrogen: The most common substance in the universe. It is usually found in the form of a gas.

Keel: The lower part of a ship. The constellation Carina (the Keel) was once part of the much larger constellation Argo Navis (the Ship *Argo*). In mythology, this was the ship in which Jason sailed to find the Golden Fleece.

Light-year: The unit of length used by astronomers to express distances to stars and other objects. It is the distance light travels in a year — about six trillion miles (9.5 trillion km)!

Magnitude: The term that astronomers use to describe the brightness of stars or other objects in the sky.

Matter: Material that takes up space and can be detected by one or more senses.

Meteor: The streak of light in the sky created by matter which has entered the Earth's atmosphere and which burns up; also the matter itself in such a case.

Meteorite: Matter which enters the atmosphere and which is large enough to survive the fall to Earth.

Meteoroid: A bit of matter passing through space. If it enters Earth's atmosphere, it becomes a fiery meteor. If it survives the fall to Earth, it becomes a meteorite.

Milky Way: The faint band of light seen crossing the sky. It is made up from the glow of thousands of stars which lie along the main plane of our Galaxy.

Mythology: Traditional stories told by ancient peoples to explain their origin and history, as well as the universe and the unknown. Much mythology formed part of the religions of these peoples.

Navigation: Directing the course of a ship or other craft.

Nuclear fusion: Energy that comes from the nuclear, or central, regions of atoms that are forced together. The Sun's heat and light come from nuclear fusion.

Observatory: A building, usually housing a telescope, from where astronomers study the sky.

Orbit: The path of an object as it travels around another; also, to travel in such a way. The Earth orbits the Sun.

Payload: In space flight, the passengers, crew, instruments, or equipment carried by a spacecraft.

Phase: In astronomy, the apparent shape of the Moon or a planet as seen from Earth, such as a crescent Moon or a full Moon.

Planet: One of the nine main members of the Sun's family.

Prominences: Huge masses of glowing gas, mainly hydrogen, which rise from the surface of the Sun.

Quasars: Very distant and very luminous objects, now known to be at the centers of galaxies emitting a great deal of energy.

Radiation: Energy given out by objects. Light and heat rays are both types of radiation. So are x-rays, gamma rays, and radio waves. The Sun, stars, and other objects in the sky give off many different kinds of radiation.

Radio telescope: A special type of telescope designed to pick up radio waves from stars and other objects in the sky.

Radio wave: See **Radiation**.

Red giant: A large star which is very bright.

Reflector: A type of telescope which uses a specially shaped mirror to collect light.

Refractor: A type of telescope which uses a lens to collect light.

Satellite: A small object orbiting a larger one. For example, artificial satellites orbit Earth. Many of the planets, including Earth, have one or more natural satellites, or moons, orbiting them.

Solar system: The system of planets, asteroids, comets, and other objects orbiting the Sun.

Space probe: A spacecraft sent by scientists and astronomers to examine planets and other objects at close range.

Stars: Hot, luminous balls of gas which appear to us as twinkling points of light in the sky.

Supernova: A colossal explosion which marks the death of a very massive star.

Telescope: A device used by astronomers for looking at stars and other objects in the sky.

Vacuum: An area which contains little or no matter of any kind.

Volume: The amount of room taken up by something.

White dwarf: A small, very dense star which is nearing the end of its life.

Year: The time it takes for the Earth, or other planets, to orbit the Sun. An Earth year is 365 1/4 days long, while a year on Pluto lasts 248 Earth years! This is how long it takes Pluto to travel around the Sun! (See **Calendar**.)

Index

A **boldface** number shows that the entry is illustrated on that page. The same page often has text about the entry, too.